FREED

A guide to

BREAKING

THE

CYCLE

OF

ABUSE

NICOLA DEANE

Disclaimer

Although the publisher and the author have made every effort to ensure that the information in this book was correct at press time and while this publication is designed to provide accurate information in regard to the subject matter covered, the publisher and the author assume no responsibility for errors, inaccuracies, omissions, or any other inconsistencies herein and hereby disclaim any liability to any party for any loss, damage, or disruption caused by errors or omissions, whether such errors or omissions result from negligence, accident, or any other cause.

This publication is meant as a source of valuable information for the reader, however it is not meant as a substitute for direct expert assistance. If such level of assistance is required, the services of a competent professional should be sought.

Dedication

This book is dedicated to all those who have been abused. No matter what level of abuse you have faced. This book is meant to empower, inspire and inform those who have faced trauma and my aim is to provide a testament that you do not need to tolerate abuse. You can live the life you truly want.

Contents

Acknowledgement

I want to thank Pastor Lorita and Pastor Gary, who have both counselled me throughout my journey to realise my full potential. Regardless of the highs and lows we have experienced, you continue to show me, with love and respect, what a true family should be.

And to the women I spent time with on the Breaking the Silence course, who have been supportive and caring throughout the duration of my healing. You have all been an inspiration that has led me to want to help others.

"I am not what has happened to me. I am what I choose to become."

-C.G. Jung

Part 1

My Story

Chapter 1

Unable To Gain A Mother's Love

I am an only child born into a Christian household to a single teenaged mother. I lived with my grandmother and mother in Birmingham for a number of years and my childhood was a strict one. My home was a harsh environment, with regular shouting. Discipline was doled out regularly by means of severe beatings with a thick rod that my grandmother called a 'busscock'. I have no idea where the name came from, but I recall a time when I mentioned to my mother that I used an empty perfume spray bottle for a science project at school and I was met with the nasty rod that left me bruised and scarred for weeks. I would lie to my teachers and blame my cat for the whip marks. My mum and grandma took the biblical phrase "spare the rod and spoil the child" quite literally and they felt that harsh physical discipline was a solid parenting technique. In later years I discovered the term was taken out of context.

I was a naturally inquisitive child, with dark eyes and curly hair. But my actions were restricted. It was drummed into me not to speak up, not to question, but be submissive and quiet. I wasn't given validation or support, but rather constant correction and discipline. The only time I received attention was when I did something wrong. I got no help with homework and was deemed a failure in school.

I quickly became accustomed to verbal abuse. I was called stupid, told I couldn't do anything, and that I would never amount to anything in life and that I was nothing. At the age of six I renamed myself Nothing. I was told that my mother wanted to abort me, because she was a teenager who didn't plan to have children. Although she was emotionally distant, I was desperate for her love and approval. I tried everything I could to please her, which cemented my skills as a people pleaser, a bad habit that led me into some bad situations.

At primary school I was bullied by a boy who thought he could physically and verbally abuse me. When I told my mum about it, she spoke to the boy's mother. I watched the conversation from a distance. The boy's mother appeared aggressive.

"In future, you will fight your own battles," my mum told me when she had finished talking to the other mother. At seven years old, I had to fend for myself. There was no support from the one person who was supposed to protect me.

Months later I found myself in situation with a teenage girl who came from a children's home. She was being cared for by a family friend. When they came to visit, she wanted to play in my room while the grownups talked. There she removed my clothing and molested me. I didn't know that it was molestation. I wasn't taught that being touched inappropriately by others was wrong. Knowing that I had to fight my own battles, I didn't say anything about the incident. And I remained silent for many years.

At the age of 14, I attended high school. A French teacher saw my vulnerability and took advantage by touching me inappropriately. At this point I shared my experience with my mother and to my disbelief she blamed me, saying that I encouraged the situation. There was no support from my mother, so I reached out to the head of year and he didn't believe me either. I was stuck attending school feeling uncomfortable, trying to avoid a teacher who touched young girls.

During my high school years I was bullied because my hair was unkempt; girls would pull my hair and demean me. There were weeks when I walked to school with broken shoes, the soles having come unstuck. My mother ignored my need for new shoes and refused to buy me a new pair. I wasn't aware that I was neglected, but my mother expressed later that she purposely did it. The neglect of my appearance led to other children calling me ugly. As you can imagine, this drastically affected my self-esteem.

The older I got, the more abuse I received. When my mum had a bad day at work, she would take her anger and frustration out on me. I would be met with pulled hair, bloodshed, and scars when sharp objects were thrown at my face. I walked on eggshells, always afraid that I would do something wrong.

In my teenage years my mother compared her looks to mine. She'd say things like, "You're prettier than me." Little did I know that I had a severely dysfunctional relationship with her. For 30 years I was unaware that the way she treated me constituted abuse. My dysfunctional upbringing created warped beliefs of love that enabled me to remain in abusive relationships later on.

As for my father, we didn't have a relationship because my mother created a divide between us by saying negative things about him. When my father asked to see me, she denied him all visits and didn't allow me to spend any time with him. My father entered an early grave; he committed suicide at the age of 45. He left a note saying there was no hope for him.

Parent-child psychology

Children, whether they are planned or not, require love, care and safety as the foundation for a happy future. Once a child has been exposed to unfortunate events at a young age, they become untrusting, insecure and unstable.

The first relationship you are supposed to have is with your mother. When a baby is born, the nurse puts the baby onto the mother's chest to create a bond. If that bond with a primary care giver and nurturer fails, the child will become confused and experience problems with his or her self-esteem later in life.

Mothers who lack love for their children usually have a bad experience during pregnancy or childbirth. In my mother's case, her pregnancy was tainted when my father got another girl pregnant at the same time. She associated me with this bad experience, so she couldn't love me.

If there are negative experiences that aren't acknowledged and dealt with, there is a high possibility that a mother will fail to form an emotional bond with her child.

According to psychologist Francine Shapiro[3*], the following list gives some examples of why parents are unable to love their children.

- An unwanted pregnancy

- Financial strain during the pregnancy

- Mother experienced abuse, or problems with her relationship during pregnancy

- Relationship problems where the mother and father separated before or after the birth

- Mother moved location before or soon after birth

- The child was a twin or triplet

- Mother was addicted to drugs or alcohol

- Mother experienced miscarriage before carrying a baby to term

- Mother experienced a family loss within two years of the birth

- Mother suffered emotional problems during pregnancy or after the birth

- Mother may feel the child got in the way of their career

- Fathers also fail to bond with their child, often because of their own experiences of childhood.

- ***Examples include:***

- The father has a bad mental image of himself which extends to his child

- The father may be immature and not want to take responsibility for his child

- The father may have unresolved trauma in his life

- The father may feel that he doesn't have anything in common with his child

Children are shaped by their environment, which impacts their self-esteem. Their interactions with others in their household give them an insight to how much they are loved and cared for. These interactions later reflect in the partners they choose and how they feel they should be treated.

When a child realises her mother or father does not have an emotional connection with her, she automatically thinks she's not good enough, is unlovable because her parents do not love her. When she grows up, she will try to find love and acceptance in all the wrong places. However, when she learns to recognise that the problem does not lie with her, she must learn to love herself first before entering a relationship.

If your parents or caregivers were emotionally distant, this book will provide tools to help you build your self-esteem, move forward, and break the repetitive cycle of dysfunctional friendships and relationships.

Chapter 2

A Toxic Friendship

In my twenties I tried to pursue an acting career. I was at the stage in my life where I wanted to build confidence in myself and finally pursue a career that I actively wanted to do. I starred in previous theatre plays where I was told regularly that I impacted many people with the characters I portrayed, so I felt with this new opportunity auditioning for The Nutcracker was a stepping stone toward a professional acting career. I attended the auditorium where I was greeted by a lady who wrote the play. I was given 10 minutes to perform as Michelle Obama and when I finished my audition, I was told that I was selected for the role. The writer introduced me to the young black male who was cast as Barak Obama. He looked at me strangely. He seemed to have recognised me from somewhere, and when we started chatting, I realised that Alex and I attended the same youth camp in Wales 15 years earlier. I had a serious crush on him at the time, and it was mutual. Because of my low self-esteem I was absolutely flattered by his attention. We spent a few minutes making out in a toilet stall one afternoon while the rest of the camp was at dinner. The camp leaders realised I was missing and sent a search party out to find me. When we heard people calling my name, we immediately returned to camp, not expecting to get caught. However, as we exited the cubicle, we ran into one of the search parties. The kids were horrified to see a young church girl leaving the toilets with a boy.

I was so happy to see Alex again, excited that we would be working together closely as Mr and Mrs Obama. We had many scenes together, and he suggested that we rehearse at his house. I accepted and we arranged to meet one evening in November. Once inside, I saw deep punch holes in the walls – a bright red clue about his character, but I ignored it. We sat in his living room, catching up over drinks. I didn't feel all that comfortable but, being polite, I listened and hung out with him. Later that evening, he boldly took off my shoes and I asked what he was doing.

"I want to massage your feet, and as you're a lady I want to give you my undivided attention," he said.

I felt uncomfortable with this gesture but I didn't say anything. He complimented my feet and then got up and sat next to me on the arm of the chair. I became tense. He moved in close and kissed my ear. I moved away and asked what he was doing.

"I'm trying to make you feel comfortable," he said.

I was bewildered. I gathered my shoes and told him I wanted to go home. He encouraged me to stay longer, but I insisted that I wanted to leave. I put my shoes on and grabbed my coat. I walked towards the door saying, "Good bye and thank you for having me". Suddenly he barricaded the front door, refusing to let me out. I didn't understand why he wouldn't let me leave, but I calmly and patiently asked him to open the door. He didn't. After many polite requests, I then forced my way passed him to grab the door handle. Alex, being a strong male, pinned me against the wall and aggressively tugged at my trousers trying to strip me. I pushed him off and reached for the door and I was finally free.

Why didn't you let me leave your house when I wanted to? I asked him in a text from the safety of my flat.

Alex responded, *I didn't want you to leave because I was enjoying your company.*

Pinning me against the wall is unacceptable, and I won't be going back to your house anymore. In future, we are going to rehearse at the theatre and I want to keep our friendship professional.

I am sorry, I won't do that again! I promise. I went too far and I don't want to lose you as a friend again.

I replied back, *Okay.*

I forgave Alex and we stayed friends. Unfortunately he took advantage of me later on.

In December, I found a new apartment, which was a positive chapter for me. I was busy attending rehearsals and preparing items for my new home. I shared the news with Alex, because I was so excited. He asked whether I needed help, but I said that I had all the help I needed.

On the day of the move, however, the removal men I was relying on didn't arrive. I couldn't move by myself so I took Alex up on his offer to help. He helped move heavy items from my childhood home into my car with my mother looking on, cold and unfriendly. While Alex helped remove my belongings, I was unaware that he was analysing the relationship between me and my mother, noting its non-existence.

After collecting the items from my old home, we met my friend

Stacey, whose grandfather was donating some things to my new apartment he didn't need after being moved into a care home. I introduced Stacey to Alex and I watched her first impressions of him. I could tell that she felt uncomfortable around him, and believed him strange due to the weird conversations he started, along with frequent interruptions. I found it amusing at the time. But looking back, this was a man who showed signs of being mentally unwell.

The three of us spent hours unpacking boxes at my new apartment, but after Stacey left, things with Alex unravelled. He asked me if I wanted to be his girlfriend, but I said that I just wanted to be friends, which he seemed to accept without a fuss. Later that evening, I was zoned out in front of the TV, exhausted from a full day of activity, when Alex suddenly stormed out of the bathroom, saying that I was ignoring his attempts to catch my attention. He started to swear and become aggressive when I told him that I just hadn't heard him calling me. When I asked him why he was behaving like this, he didn't respond.

"You were ignoring me," he repeated.

When I tried to explain my side of the story, he stormed out of the apartment. His behaviour confused me. I called my cousin Sarah, who was living in London at the time, wanting to tell her about the strange situation. A few moments later, Alex knocked on the apartment door. I looked at him through the keyhole.

"I want to go home," he said.

"You can go home. The buses are running," I responded.

"My home is too far away and I don't have any bus money," he replied.

I took pity on him and allowed him back into the apartment, at which point he demanded that I take him home.

"With that tone and attitude I will not take you anywhere," I told him.

He sat down on the floor, in the middle of the living room, demanding to be taken home. I was thoroughly confused. There was a grown man sitting on my floor, making demands and behaving like a child.

Sarah was still on the phone, listening to the conversation. When I told Alex that he was acting like a child, his demeanour changed quickly. He got up and grabbed my throat.

"If you won't take me home, I'll take your car keys," he said.

He released my throat then quickly took the keys. I made a grab for the keys, but I wasn't fast enough. Alex spotted my bank card on the kitchen counter and put it into his pocket. I had no choice but to fight for my things. While I was trying to defend myself, he pinned me against the door, spat in my face and called me derogatory names. He repeatedly slapped me around the face and tore off my clothes. He sexually assaulted me and I broke down crying.

Alex stood in front of me smiling. He felt powerful, having succeeded in assaulting me and making me cry. He heard noises from my phone and he put it to his ear. My cousin told him that she heard everything and would call the police. He ended the call, grabbed a knife from the kitchen counter and said he was ready to kill anyone who came near him. He locked himself in my living room, waiting for the police to arrive. I ran to my bedroom, locking myself inside. I was scared of his plans and didn't know if I was going to leave my apartment alive.

After hours of being held hostage, Alex demanded that I drive him to the cash machine to withdraw my money. At that point I feared for my life and didn't know what to expect from him, so I complied. I had £30 available in my account so he withdrew the funds and pressured me into calling him a taxi to take him home. He sent me a text later that night, apologising for his behaviour, and threatening to kill me if I reported what had happened to the police. I believed him. I told my friends about the incident and they encouraged me to contact the police and press charges. Months later CPS dropped the charges due to lack of evidence.

When I told the theatre group about how Alex attacked me, they revealed that Alex was full of hate towards women because his mother abandoned him and he was raised in a children's home. Many other women had rejected him over the years; I was the latest one to turn down his advances, and it made him angry. So he lashed out, physically attacking me.

Abusers often blame their adult behaviour on their childhood or upbringing. Many of them were abused or neglected. But these are just excuses. Adults choose how they want to behave.

Chapter 3

Toxic Aunty

My father's sister was an inconsistent presence in my life. I remember her being around for a short time when I was a young child, but she disappeared for a long time after that. When my grandmother passed away in 2016, I was 29. My aunt learned of her passing and took my number from one of my grandmother's friends, wanting to reinitiate a relationship with me.

We got off to a great start. I would visit her £1.5 million home that consisted of six bedrooms, three bathrooms, a games room, gym, two dining rooms, and a large open-plan kitchen that looked out over the 50-acre park-like garden. She confided in me that her husband had left her after 22 years for a younger woman, and how she might lose her home due to financial difficulties. I wanted to make her feel happy and loved, so I would treat her to meals and surprised her with gifts.

A year later when I lost my apartment, my aunt kindly invited me to live with her and her family for five months while I looked for a new place of my own. I trusted her and felt we had built a stable relationship, so I felt comfortable moving into her large, expensive home in Coventry with my grandfather and three cousins. I felt like I was recovering lost family members, which made me happy.

A few weeks before moving into my aunt's home I unexpectedly suffered from an angina attack. On top of that, an infection entered my heart and I was admitted to hospital. During this challenging time, my boyfriend David supported and cared for me. My aunt, hearing of his good deeds, would praise him and even invited him round for dinner with the rest of the family. But as soon as my aunt analysed David's odd behaviour during family gatherings, their relationship deteriorated. David believed my aunt would try to control me and before I moved into her home, he was concerned that he was going to lose me. I reassured him that she couldn't force me to break up with him. My love for him wouldn't allow anyone to separate us. He was strongly against the move, but I did it anyway.

As I unpacked my things in my new room, I felt at home, like I belonged to a family again. In the evenings, my aunt would cook for the family and we would sit around a large marble dinner table discussing our day. For the first few days, I settled in nicely and I attended my work shifts at a customer call centre as usual. Within a week, though, I noticed some odd behaviours.

One evening, when I returned home from work, I decided to sit with my grandfather in the living quarters where he would regularly watch television. I entered the large open kitchen space where my aunt was watching television and I said hello to her. I told her that I was going to sit with my grandfather for a short while, keeping him company.

"You don't need to sit with him. He doesn't like people," she told me.

I ignored this comment, and spent a few hours with him.

When I saw my aunt later that evening, she sat me down for a talk.

"Who do you think you are?" she asked.

"Pardon?" I responded, confused.

"You are treating me like I am the receptionist of this house. Who do you think you are? You come in and you say hello, then say you're going to sit with grandad, who said I didn't want to talk! I wanted to know how your day went! That was what I was expecting!" Her harsh tone and chastisement reduced me to tears.

Although I didn't say anything to her, I felt that I was spending more than enough time with my aunt every evening, watching her favourite TV shows. I wondered to myself, "If I'm crying already – one week in – how will I manage five more months here?"

Things only got worse. I was informed that my aunt wanted everyone home, with the door locked behind them, by 5pm every day. Apparently this eased her anxiety. But it gave me no opportunity to meet friends or to do a hobby after work. And if I wasn't home, she would phone me immediately to find out what I was doing. By December, less than a month into my stay, I was feeling very restricted, but I had to adhere to the rules because I had nowhere else to live.

One evening, my aunt confronted me about David. She disliked him and wanted me to find someone else.

"A pretty girl like you, I can imagine a hulk coming to the door and whisking you away. What on earth did you see in David? He is scrawny and has no money, no ambition! His family is trailer park trash," she said.

I gave a slight smile and nod. She continued. "Nicola, you're prettier than me! The world is your oyster!"

I lead her to believe that I dumped David, which earned her respect. She was happy to think that I was looking for a better man.

But I would still see David right after finishing work. We would meet at the nearest coffee shop and I would express my concerns about living at the house. The control my aunt was exerting over my life was becoming overwhelming. I was desperate to have my freedom back, to live in my own apartment. He suggested that we start looking at apartments in the New Year. Despite how unhappy I was living with my aunt, secretly looking for apartments made me feel guilty.

My aunt's control became unbearable. I couldn't even choose my own clothes. On Christmas Eve, she forced me to change out of a fluffy grey jumper that I loved, into a horrid orange one for a meal out with the family. I didn't want to fight, so I changed. But I wondered what else she would try to control. Our relationship really started breaking down at this point.

I tried to be helpful, but nothing I did seemed enough. At a family gathering the day after Christmas, she began treating me like a servant, regularly telling me to top up everyone's wine glasses. Even my cousins were talking to me like a waitress and I had enough of being treated like a stranger. So I decided to sit among everyone else.

My aunt then told a story of an encounter she had with a neighbour.

"I was heading to the park for a jog, and bumped into my neighbour. She asked me how I am keeping since my husband has left me. She mentioned the car on the drive, asking if I have found someone new. I looked at her startled. I mean, how could she think I'd be with someone who drives a blue Peugeot?"

Everyone laughed hysterically. I couldn't see what was so funny. The next day, I confronted her.

"Aunty, when you said that you'd never be with someone who drives a blue Peugeot, what do you mean?"

"I would never find myself with a man driving a car like yours," she explained. "Your cousins are grabbing life by the throat, opening many businesses. But you, in a customer services job… you are down there." She waved her hand close to the floor.

Suddenly, I'd had enough. "I haven't said anything about the way you've been treating me, but I'm sick of biting tongue. I don't appreciate you telling me how to speak and what to wear. And now you insult me by saying my life is 'down there' and compare me to my cousins."

She didn't reply to my comment, but changed the subject. "Can I have your mother's telephone number please?" she responded.

I was caught off guard, and without thinking, I gave her my mother's telephone number.

She then responded, "Nicola, I think you are over exaggerating and I want to speak with your mother."

I felt overwhelmed and couldn't contain the tears that poured down my face. I stormed out of the kitchen and grabbed my coat. I jumped into my car and drove to David's house and told him what had happened.

A few minutes later my phone pinged. My aunt had sent me a message.

What you have done to me is not fair. How could you?

I couldn't figure out what she meant, and I didn't reply. After the message came a string of calls that I didn't answer. Eventually I sent her a text.

I am leaving the house and will find a new apartment.

When she called again, I answered my phone.

"You are leaving the house?" she demanded.

"Yes," I replied.

"How can you do this to me?" she screeched in a high-pitched, hysterical tone.

"I don't know what you mean. What am I doing to you?"

"You're leaving me here all alone. I helped you and you do all this to me!"

I really didn't understand why she was so upset. But I laid out my plan for her, so that there was no confusion.

"I want to leave the house, and I will not be returning tonight. I will be staying with a friend. And I won't be attending the New Year's Eve party you invited me to."

At this news, she ended the call.

I told David about the conversation and he advised me to be careful because she could attack me. I decided to stay away from the house for a few nights. While I was away, my aunt texted me.

Come back here.

I need you to come back.

I was mildly concerned and asked if everything was okay.

I want you to come back.

I took her texts to mean that she wanted to make amends, resolve the conflict. Even so, I really didn't want to see her. Going against my gut instinct I returned to her house.

Meanwhile my aunt sent her kids to stay with their father for a few days.

When I knocked on the door at 6.30pm, my aunt was on the phone. I assumed she was talking to a friend. As I passed by her into the house, I heard her say, "I live with my elderly dad and three boys and I can't take it no more."

I didn't think anything of the comment and continued up the stairs into my room.

"So you are not going to the New Year's Eve ball then?" my aunt asked, storming into the room.

I was sitting on the bed and looked up at her. "No, because my cousins are going and I know you think they are better than me, so I don't see the point".

She started getting angry and pushed me flat onto the bed. She told me that she had been drinking all day.

"Why are you pushing me?" I asked, not understanding why she was behaving so aggressively.

I got up off the bed to gather my belongings, but she pushed me back down.

"So you like to fight?" she said.

"No," I said. "What are you doing?"

"Your mother told me you like to fight!" she told me.

I didn't realise it at the time that, she had been on the phone to my mother when I arrived. I flashed back to subtle hints that my mum had given me previously. "If I was you, I would leave the house," she had said. Then I realised that my mother was an accessory to my aunts plan to attack me.

I struggled to get up from the bed again.

"If you get up again, I am going to punch you in your face!" she threatened.

I got back up, and a fist charged toward my face, hitting me in my eye socket. We immediately began tussling. I pushed her off me. She forced me back onto the bed and held me down. I instantly kicked her in the stomach. She grabbed my hair and I looked for my phone that was lost in the sheets on the bed. She fell onto the bed, continued to grab my hair and used her hands to strangle me. I was still searching blindly for my phone to call someone for help. I was struggling to breathe, but I was able to bite her hard on her leg. Thankfully, she loosened her grip on my throat and I sucked in a deep breath. She let go of my hair and I continued to chase after my phone.

My glasses had been knocked off and I was covered in blood. I was desperate to leave the house, but I needed help. I finally found my phone and rang David. The call went to voicemail and I left a message. Then I rang my friend Stacey. She answered and I screamed down the phone, asking her to collect me at the house. I was still trapped on the bed, my aunt listening to the telephone conversation. She reached for the drinking glass on a chest of drawers and threw it at my face. I screamed for Stacey to come to my aid. I rang David again and he finally answered the phone. I urgently asked him to come to the house and mentioned that I was being physically attacked by my aunt. As if to prove a point, my aunt punched and kicked me while I was talking to David. When she got tired of fighting, she stood back and watched me gather up my belongings. After I had placed my clothes into a suitcase, she kicked my clothes all over the room.

My grandfather heard the screaming from upstairs over the blare of the TV. He came to investigate, saw his daughter kicking my belongings into the hallway, and went to his bedroom. He completely ignored the whole situation, and certainly didn't care about my wellbeing. My aunty continued to kick and spit on my belongings, then brought out a knife and pointed it at my stomach. I stood still for long minutes that felt like hours. She was threatening to kill me when Stacey and her mother knocked on the front. My grandfather rushed to answer the door and my aunt hid the knife while Stacey and her mother climbed the stairs to see the mess scattered in my room and in the hallway.

"Let's go!" I said to Stacey, collecting my clothing off the floor.

But Stacey and her mum didn't want to leave. They wanted to know what was going on. My aunt took the opportunity to win the ladies over.

"Nicola has been leaving the room a mess and I'm tired of the state of the house," she told them. I gave her a disbelieving look, but continued to pack my things.

David finally arrived, banging loudly on the front door.

"Who is that?" my aunt wanted to know.

Stacey checked out the window. "David."

Neither Stacey nor my aunt liked David and they rushed down the stairs, but not before my aunty grabbed a block of wood from a broken mirror frame. My grandfather opened the door and David angrily pushed his way into the house, shouting. Stacey grabbed the chunk of wood from my aunt and threw it at David's head, but she missed. The two women push David out of the house, then they evicted me the same way. I tumbled down the front doorsteps. Some of my possessions were unceremoniously thrown out after me, but I was locked out of the house and not allowed to collect the rest of my stuff.

Stacey remained with my aunt while her mother collected my things. It was clear that Stacey had sided with my aunt, and I broke off our friendship.

During the incident my aunt told me not to go to the police, and initially I didn't. A few days later I changed my mind and pressed charges, but the police told me that since there were no witnesses and no evidence, I didn't have a case. My aunt claimed that I started the fight, and the whole thing was just a case of 'she said, she said'.

Over time I realised that my aunt was a master manipulator who claimed she was the victim. She planned to ruin my life by using my friends, relatives, and the clergy against me. Somehow, she got the idea that she could control my life and might even have the chance to murder me. She had insecurities along with unresolved pain, which she projected onto me, trying to demean me and break my confidence.

Chapter 4

Breaking Free From The Cycle Of Abuse

The start of my discovery toward breaking free started when I was introduced to my pastor by my friend Laura. Laura was aware that my pastor counselled women who have been through trauma.

Forgiveness

In my first session I briefly told my pastor about the dysfunctional relationship I had with my mother, and she told me she could see that I hadn't forgiven her. I strongly disagreed and believed I had forgiven my mother. I received counselling for five years and my pastor taught me about true forgiveness and loving others as Jesus does.

Self-worth

I recall an exercise that I did with my pastor. She asked me if a million pounds was scrunched and thrown onto the floor would it be of value or not? I said no. She said the correct answer is, just because the million pounds was screwed up it still has value of a million pounds. This example was an eye opener as it made me realised that I based my worth on how others have treated me.

Healthy relationships

One of our counselling sessions stood out to me – I explained in depth about my childhood. As my pastor listened, she revealed that I was raised unhealthy. I was under the impression that my childhood was normal. During that particular session we looked at friendships and relationships, and what they should look like. We discussed at length what self-worth was she and taught me how to set boundaries.

Breaking the silence

After attending counselling for several years, a timely opportunity came along for a six-month course called Breaking the Silence, founded and coordinated by Raj Holiness. My pastor encouraged me to attend. And I'm so glad that I did; this course was the turning point to changing my life!

I attended the course which is aimed at abused women, children and anyone who has experienced domestic abuse, forced marriage and human trafficking to start the recovery from traumatic experiences.

I was put into a class with four other women and the course covered the following topics: love, identity, personal care, health, facing fears, success, freedom and breakthrough. We were given a journal that contained self-reflection questions that enabled me to learn more about myself. The journal was a great way for me to journal my thoughts and the self-reflection questions were thought provoking and brought inner healing.

I attended fortnightly group sessions focusing on each of the topics mentioned above. And we had to participate in games and activities that all contained a powerful message of how to break the cycle of abuse.

In that six-month period I learned so much about myself. I finally understood what love should look like, and how to heal from the past and move forward with no guilt or shame.

The course made such a huge impact on my life that friends started to see a change in my behaviour and noticed that I appeared more confident in how I interacted with others.

At the end of the course, I learned how to put boundaries into action with those who were abusing my trust, and I learned that I could choose what type of people I wanted in my life.

The course provided a freedom action plan for my financial, living, work, relationship and personal goals. I ended the course feeling empowered and having much to look forward to.

In our final session there were different words laid on a table and we each had to pick three words each. I chose the following words to live by:adventure, happiness, and honesty.

Reflection on my life

As I reflected, I realised that I didn't love myself which is why I ignored the warning signs I saw in others. I ignored how I felt when others mistreated me. I didn't create boundaries. I carried anger and a distaste for life under the surface. While I was carrying these hidden feelings around with me, I was unaware that I was attracting a similar type of person in friendships and relationships.

I noticed that I never had a successful relationship, and the people in my life were using or abusing me. So, from this evaluation I started to analyse each experience and think about what I could have done to prevent it from happening again.

After 30 years of abuse, I can now say that I am living abuse-free, a life of peace and harmony surrounded by good people. I have reached this point by implementing boundaries, building my self-esteem and being aware of any toxic behaviours.

I have learned from my past experiences, and I am more selective of the friends and formal relationships that I accept in my life. I choose friends based on commonalities, whether we are both compatible with our values and life goals, and I am vigilant about how they treat me (e.g. their attitude towards me if I mention any success). I have developed a list of questions (which you'll find in Chapter 12) that I use to assess my relationships. This list is not exhaustive, but it will give you a guideline of things to look for in a person's behaviour if you meet a new friend or potential partner.

I have successfully steered clear of the abusive cycle for many years now, but I remain on alert for abusive behaviour. If I feel that a relationship or friendship is harming me on any level, I will discuss my concerns with the person. If I find that the person is intentionally trying to harm me, I will create a distance between us. That is what Breaking the Silence course taught me.

Part 2

Recognising Abuse

Chapter 5

Different Types Of Abuse

In order to break the cycle of abuse, you must be aware of what abuse is.

Definition of Abuse

Abuse is defined as cruel and violent treatment of a person or animal. Abuse has various forms such as physical abuse, sexual abuse, emotional abuse and verbal abuse.

While you are in a relationship with someone, whether a friend or a romantic partner, if you feel afraid to speak your truth and purposely change your behaviour to avoid any lasting consequences, then this is a sign that you are being abused.

According to The First Step organisation, the following are examples of abuse.

Different types of abuse

Social media abuse

 All types of social media can attract 'keyboard warriors' who type mean or cruel comments online, without having to reveal their identity.

Examples include:

- Bullying individuals online about their race, religious beliefs, body image, skin colour, etc.

- Harassment

- Intimidation

- Threats

- Pressures to send explicit videos

- Put-downs using status updates

- Constant direct messages

- Try to damage your reputation online

- Setting up profiles in your mane

- Cyber stalking

- Stealing your identity

- Revenge porn - uploading explicit material of you

- Digital spying

- Encouraging others to join in to the abuse

Emotional abuse

 Emotional abuse can come from anyone – relatives, partners, friends, co-workers and employers. This type of abuse aims to lower another's confidence using verbal statements.

Examples include:

- Intimidation and threats

- Shouting

- Acting aggressively

- Making you feel scared

- Harsh criticism

- Name calling

- Constant insults

- Undermining your self-worth

- Sarcastic or unpleasant comments

- Undermining your opinion

- Being really nice after being cruel

- Emotional blackmail

- Suicide threats

- Silent treatment

- Character assassination

- Swearing

- Being patronising

- Public embarrassment

- Dismissiveness – head shaking, eye rolling and sighing

- Trying to make you look foolish

- Insulting your appearance

- Belittling your accomplishments

- Put downs of your interests

- Ignoring you

- Destroying your personal items or taking them away intentionally

- Blaming you for their disappointments and problems

- Pushing your buttons

- Not allowing you to express how you feel

- Gas lighting – when the other person makes you feel that your emotions aren't reasonable and claims that you are blowing a situation out of proportion, leading you to second-guess yourself

- Breaching court orders and not allowing you to see your children

This list is by no means complete, so if you are unsure whether you are being emotionally abused, examine how a person makes you feel. If someone refuses to listen to your concerns, or doesn't allow you to express your feelings, you're likely experiencing emotional abuse. If you feel scared or small due to other people's behaviour, its abusive behaviour.

Other examples of emotional abuse:

- ☉ "If you don't do this, you don't love me."

- ☉ "I'm not attracted to you anymore because I've been seeing other women who are more attractive than you."

- ☉ "You aren't a quick learner, and because of that I'm choosing Rachel as the supervisor instead of you."

- ☉ Being called stupid and/or being compared to other family members or colleagues.

Sexual abuse

Sexual abuse is defined as unwanted or abusive sexual behaviour by one person upon another. It is often perpetrated using force or by taking advantage of another. Sexual abuse can happen to anyone from a child to an adult, and can occur clothed or unclothed.

The intension of the abuser is to lord power over the victim, making the abuser feel superior.

Examples include:

- ☉ Forcing the victim to perform sexual acts without consent

- ☉ Being forced to undress

- ☉ Any unwanted touching

- ☉ Unwanted kissing

- Unwanted fondling

- Pinching or biting breasts

- Enforcing prostitution

- Using sexual objects that cause harm

- Rape

- Being exposed to someone who is performing a sexual act

- Forcing the victim to copy pornographic acts

- Unwanted videoing/photography while performing sexual acts

- Flashing

- Deliberately causing pain during sex

- Using sexually degrading insults

- Unwanted exposure to pornography

- Sexual jokes

- Withholding sex as punishment

- Using sex to coerce compliance

- Manipulating the victim to have sex in exchange for money or other necessities

- Forcing someone to have sex with others

- Human trafficking

Physical abuse

Physical abuse is defined as non-accidental use of force that results in bodily injury, pain, or impairment.

Examples include:

- Hitting and slapping on any area of the body

- Punching and kicking

- Pinching, scratching and biting

- Shaking and suffocating

- Strangling

- Pulling hair

- Scalding or burning

- Spitting

- Forcing you to swallow anything that endangers or harms you

- Pushing and shoving

- Using any weapon to attack the other person

- Pulling or ripping off clothes

- Force feeding

- Withholding food or medical attention

- Breaking bones

- Drugging or poisoning

- Restraining

- Drowning

- Cutting flesh

- Being denied sleep

- Murder

- Organ trafficking

- Forced labour

Financial abuse

 The Care Act 2014 describes financial abuse as a type of abuse which includes having money or other property stolen, being defrauded, being put under pressure in relation to money or other property and having money or other property misused.

Examples include:

- Theft

- Exploiting personal assets for personal gain

- Controlling your finances without consent

- Preventing you from getting a job

- Not allowing you to see bank statements, bills, or any financial

transactions

- Putting all the bills in another person's name to avoid paying them

- Withholding money or credit cards

- Receiving an insufficient allowance from a partner

- Being forced to work from home so they can keep an eye on you

- Sabotaging your job

- Setting up financial loans, credit cards, and hire purchase agreements and making you sign for them

- Preventing you from choosing your own career

- Refusing to pay bills or buy food

- Spending money that is not theirs on frivolous items or activities

- Interfering with your training, education or employment

- Maliciously preventing you from purchasing things that you want

- Making you beg for money

- Stealing your possessions or money

Non-verbal abuse

Non-verbal abuse is any form of intimidating, harassing, threatening or condescending behaviour without saying a word.

Examples include:

- Rolling eyes

- Angry facial expressions

- Tutting

- Smirking

- Whispering

- Ignoring you

- Hands on hips

- Violating personal space

- Being prohibited from going outside

- Restricting access to food, water or ablutions

- Isolating you from others

- Giving everyone in the group something beneficial and purposely withholding it you. *This behaviour is often spotted in classrooms, workplace, or team sports*

- Being purposefully irritating

- Kicking or damaging property

Spiritual abuse

 Spiritual abuse is when someone doesn't respect your spiritual beliefs and they aim to demean or harm you.

Examples include:

- Forcing you to go against your beliefs

- Forced marriage

- Threats to harm or kill in the name of honour

- Using religious or spiritual beliefs to manipulate, humiliate or embarrass you

- Denying access to a place of worship or religious ceremonies

- Using religious beliefs as an excuse for violence

- Ridiculing spiritual or religious beliefs

- Female genital mutilation

You don't need a bad childhood experience to attract abusers. Perpetrators are keenly aware of other people's vulnerabilities and will exploit them if it suits them. If you lack confidence in yourself, your success, or any other aspect of your personality or life, an abuser will pick up on this and use this against you. To break the cycle of abuse, you have to build up your confidence, develop self-love and gain the strength to walk away from anyone who tries to take advantage of you.

If you are unsure about your situation, unsure as to whether you are experiencing abuse, try imagining what advice you'd give a friend in your situation. This will help clarify your situation.

Chapter 6

Signs Of Controlling Behaviour

For some people, their insecurities make them feel the need to dominate or control others. Being in charge of people and situations makes them feel powerful. Whatever their reasons are, you can combat their behaviour by creating boundaries.

Some examples of controlling behaviours are:

⊙ Seeking more attention than others

⊙ Threatening you with ultimatums

⊙ Putting you down when things don't go their way

⊙ Telling you what to wear

⊙ Using banter as a disguise for underlying criticism in the presence of others

⊙ Making you feel unworthy or worthless

⊙ Not allowing you to have a life outside of work

⊙ Not allowing you to visit the people you want to see

⊙ Taking control of your finances

- Restricting when you leave the house and where you go

- Accusing you of lying without evidence

- Being demanding

- Constantly checking or spying on you

- Invading your privacy

- Get irrationally upset when they don't get their own way

- Persuading you to change who you are

- Blaming you for everything and not taking any responsibility

- Refusing to compromise

- Choosing your food at a restaurant

- Strict and detailed rules of expectant behaviour

- Forced marriage

- Using force to maintain power

- Monitoring your time

- Choosing who you see

- Telling you what to think

If you suspect that your partner or friend is controlling you, answer these questions to understand your situation better:

- ⊙ What are you feeling when you are in their presence? Do you feel depressed? Do you feel anxious? Do you change and become withdrawn?

- ⊙ Can you be yourself?

- ⊙ Are you allowed your freedom?

- ⊙ Do you have choices in the given circumstances?

- ⊙ Is there compromise?

- ⊙ Are you pushed aside when it comes to decision making?

- ⊙ Do they listen to and value your opinions?

If you feel trapped, restricted, dominated, concerned for your safety, or fearful, please rethink the relationship or friendship. In a healthy relationship you will feel safe, loved, valued, heard and allowed to be yourself. If you do not have these positive qualities in your relationship, you need to re-evaluate.

The cycle of abuse wheel

The abusive cycle is something that I have learned during my experience and I have created a diagram on how the abusive cycle works.

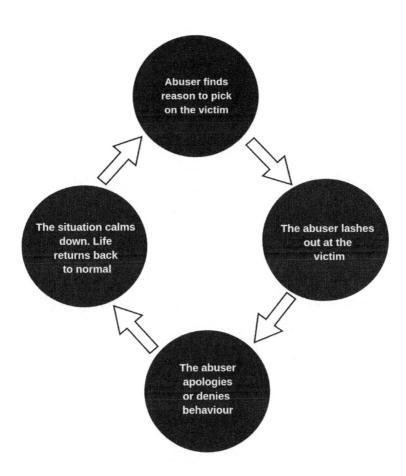

Chapter 7

Why People Do Not Leave Abusive Relationships

People often question why some people stay in an abusive relationship, or why they put up with the abuse. Oftentimes it's not easy to leave the relationship. Below are a few reasons why people chose not to leave.

⊙ **Afraid to look weak**

The victim may feel weak when they are in an abusive relationship. They feel they have no support, that others will look down on them and authorities will not believe them. So they remain in the toxic situation.

⊙ **Afraid of being murdered**

The Chief Executive of Refuge, Sandra Horley, has claimed that, in England and Wales, two women a week are killed by a current or former partner. And the numbers are rising. One in three victims are males.

⊙ **Feeling ashamed**

Men often feel ashamed of finding themselves in an abusive

relationship and fear being seen as less of a man if they report their female partners. Sexual preference and/or orientation is another factor. If the victim hasn't come out yet, they may not want to report their partner in order to keep their secret.

⊙ **In denial**

Sometimes abusers gaslight their victims, making them doubt their feelings and memories. Perpetrators usually manipulate and play around with the victim's emotions – apologising for their behaviour, or following up an act of abuse with a kind gesture. Sometimes they blame the victim for their actions, causing the victim to question their feelings.

⊙ **Afraid of losing their children**

This is more often the experience of male victims. If they take their female abuser to court, they could lose custody of, or access to, their children if the court finds in favour of the mother.

⊙ **Low self-worth**

Being told constantly that no one will ever love you breaks down your self-esteem and self-worth, and soon you begin to believe these statements are true. When you feel unlovable, you believe that the abusive relationship is all that you deserve.

⊙ **Religious beliefs**

Some religions teach that people mustn't leave the relationship for the sake of Allah, or God, or another deity.

Statistics

According to United Nations, thirty-five percent of women worldwide have experienced physical or sexual violence.

When the coronavirus pandemic lockdown started in March 2020, governments around the world advised sixty-six billion people to stay home for up to three months. Officials feared domestic abuse would rise by fifty percent. Their fears became reality, with police calls rising in the UK by forty-nine percent. Police were answering abuse related phone calls every thirty seconds and charities worldwide have been experiencing seven hundred percent more calls throughout the pandemic. The United Nations reported that domestic abuse reports in France rose by thirty percent; reports in Spain rose by eighteen percent in the first two weeks of lockdown; and China had more reports than usual, although there are no exact figures.

According to sociologists, when families spend more time together, such as over Christmas and summer vacations, there are more opportunities for domestic violence.

The *New York Times* reported that perpetrators are more likely to murder their partners in the wake of financial sets backs and lost jobs. And these statistics are expected to soar throughout the pandemic.

Refuge, a women's charity that is currently supporting six-and-a-half thousand women and children rebuild their lives from abuse, declared that one in three women aged sixteen to fifty-nine will be in an abusive relationship in their lifetime. In the UK, three women commit suicide every week because they see no other way out of an abusive relationship. Six percent of domestic abuse cases start during pregnancy.

During 2019, 1.6 million women in England and Wales experienced domestic abuse.

Women who experience domestic violence are twice as likely to experience depression and forty percent of homeless women state that violence has contributed to their circumstances. Many women who are married to an abusive spouse find it harder to leave, despite the many supportive groups and governmental bodies that will provide housing for those who feel unsafe.

Men can also become vulnerable to abuse. According to the gov.uk website, 2.4 million victims of domestic abuse a year are between the ages of sixteen and seventy-four, and 786,000 of them are men. Helpguide.org states that one in three men in the UK experience domestic abuse in heterosexual and homosexual relationships. But this figure may not be terribly accurate as men are less likely to admit to being in an abusive relationship, either because they are embarrassed by their situation or scared of their abuser.

Abuse is not confined to the home. One in four people, both men and women, have experienced workplace bullying in their lifetime. In the workplace, abuse takes the form of intimidation, humiliation, denigration, undermining a colleague or employee, intentionally offending someone, or injuring someone.

I have included abuse helplines at the end of this book. If you feel that you are in danger, please contact an organisation that will support you and provide the help needed for your circumstances.

Part 3

Begin the Healing

Chapter 8

Breaking Free

"Refuse to inherit dysfunction. Learn new ways of living instead of repeating what you lived through"

-Thema Davis

We have looked at the various types of abuse. Now we need to look at your habits and how they contribute to your situation. Think about your family of origin. What attitudes, habits, and lifestyles have they adopted throughout your lifetime that have been passed on to you? For example, when a caregiver talks negatively about him or herself, a child learns to do the same. This leads to low self-esteem. Or, if a mother has been in unstable relationships with men while her child was growing up, this breeds instability for the child. As grown-ups, these children often choose partners who perpetuate that instability because they don't know what a stable relationship looks like.

Our childhood experiences are the foundation of our future. Children learn how to interact with others by how their caregivers treat them. Some caregivers are supportive while some are abusers. The purpose of this book is to help those who were abused in the early stages of childhood learn about the subliminal patterns with which they have been living.

We cannot change something of which we are not aware, so it's important that we recognise dysfunctional patterns of behaviour in our lives in order to break free from this cycle.

To understand if you have been living in a dysfunctional cycle, look back at your childhood. Answer these questions to see if you can identify the root of any unhealthy cycles you're living with today.

How were your treated by your family, friends and teachers?

_____

_____

_____

_____

_____

_____

What negative experiences can you remember as a child, and how did they impact your outlook on life?

_____

_____

_____

_____

_____

_____

Were you living in a happy home full of love and protection, or did you live in an unloving, hostile environment?

_____

_____

_____

_____

_____

_____

_____

Were you regularly cared for?

Were you supported and praised, or criticised and put down? Try to recall all of your memories.

What negative statements were you told or believed when you were growing up? *For example, your sister is much smarter or prettier than you.*

_____

_____

_____

_____

_____

_____

_____

If you cannot identify any unhealthy behaviours, ask a trusted friend or relative, who knows your family situation and home life, who has witnessed or heard of experiences that you went through to see what patterns of behaviour they can spot.

Once you recall your experiences, question the choices you have made in your life. Has your childhood negatively impacted your choice of partners and friends?

It's easy to blame a childhood caregiver for your current circumstances, but as an adult, you become responsible for your choices, even if your upbringing predisposed you to make bad decisions. Take control of your life by recognising your thought patterns and behaviours. Then unlearn the bad behaviours by adopting a new mind-set.

Chapter 9

Applying Boundaries

"People will treat you based on how much you allow them to treat you."

-Anonymous

Between the ages of birth and seven years, we learn what is and is not acceptable behaviour, what we can do and what others can do to us. Unfortunately, those who were abused as children often believe that abuse is normal and it usually becomes a part of their everyday life. When they get older, they tend to attract unhealthy relationships where friends and partners like to test the limits to which they may abuse this person. Once an abuser spots the lack of boundaries, the victim automatically finds themselves in an abusive cycle.

You may have heard of the expression "hurt people, hurt people". And this is true. Abusers take advantage of vulnerable people, causing pain, confusion and lower the confidence of others because of how they feel about themselves. While abusers need to take responsibility for their actions, they are also people with deep rooted issues that need to be addressed.

It's important to remember that whatever abuse you have received is not a reflection of you, but rather a reflection of the abuser. Abusers have a warped sense of self and project their issues onto others. For example, a boy who was abandoned by his parents will most likely carry this insecurity through to his adult life and will interpret even unconnected actions as his partner preparing to leave him.

All relationships need boundaries. Without boundaries, you are inviting people to treat you unfairly. It's not always easy, especially with people who refuse to respect you, but once you start putting boundaries in place, the cycle of abuse will be broken.

There were many times when I should have set boundaries with my friends, boyfriends and relatives, but I was fearful of what would happen. My thoughts were:

- If I tell my partner or aunt how I feel, what will they think of me?

- Will my relationship with them change dramatically for the worse?

- If I speak up, then I may be lonely, or have no boyfriend or relatives to love and accept me.

These are usually common questions when you haven't set boundaries in your relationships. But remember, in order to have a healthy relationship it requires boundary setting to avoid hidden resentment and to maintain the peace for both parties as well as respect.

What is a boundary?

Boundaries are the limits you set that define what behaviour you find acceptable from others. Let me illustrate the concept with an analogy.

55

Imagine a house with a fence and gate around the garden. The property is clearly defined by the fence. The pavement is for the members of public to walk on. The gate is the entry point to the property, and the owner controls who may and may not enter. And once a visitor enters, the owner is responsible for how he or she behaves while visiting. If the owner doesn't stop a visitor from running around the house and breaking all the dishes, the visitor will continue with this course of action.

Children who have been brought up with poor boundaries have a difficult time setting proper boundaries for themselves, allowing the abusers in their lives to continually break dishes in their houses.

Boundaries are used to protect our mental, physical, emotional and spiritual health. We use words and actions to set boundaries. If you do not communicate your discomfort, the other person will never know how you are feeling. For example, if a work colleague talks down to you and you don't tell them how you are feeling, you will not resolve the issue, and you will let resentment fester. And the colleague will think that it is okay to behave this way towards you. Or, if your partner regularly takes money from your purse without your permission, he or she will continue to do this until you speak up about the issue.

The word no is a definite boundary marker. It informs the other person that you are uncomfortable with something, that you disagree with them, or that you would not like to participate. If the person refuses to accept a "No" from you, tries to cajole or embarrass you into participating in an activity that makes you feel uncomfortable, you have to stand firmly by your decision. Unfortunately this can become confrontational, but if you back down, you risk having your boundary compromised.

Sometimes it's scary to say no to others, but speaking up and expressing how you feel will become empowering as you practice it. Sometimes people might not like hearing our "No", but that's just human nature. You cannot please everyone. The purpose of applying boundaries is to protect yourself. If you people-please all the time, you will become resentful. It can be daunting to start creating boundaries if you have never done it before, but applying boundaries will create healthy relationships.

To maintain a boundary, you must love and respect yourself. Know how much you're willing to accept. Listen to your feelings, your gut instincts. If you're unhappy or uncomfortable, speak up. Because some people will try and push you as far as they can.

However, you must respect other people's boundaries in order for them to respect yours.

Example

Abuse can be likened to a bad experience in a restaurant. Billy and Sally plan to go to a really nice restaurant they have seen in the city that looks inviting from the outside. They wear the appropriate attire for the occasion, arrive timeously for their reservation, and are seated. They notice the table is wobbly, but ignore it and decide to remain at the table. The waiter approaches and they order. Billy notices the cutlery doesn't look as shiny and clean as he has seen at other restaurants, but overlooks it. Sally is hungry and looks around the busy restaurant, seeing people chatting, eating and enjoying their evening. She notices that she and Billy are the only ones waiting for food. After an hour, Billy asks the waiter how much longer their food will be. The waiter says that their order will be ready soon. The food finally arrives and when Sally starts eating, she discovers a long strand of black hair in her food. After waiting for an hour for her meal, and working up quite an appetite in that time, she is now put off her food. Billy informs the waiter about Sally's dinner and the waiter sends it back to the kitchen. The manager comes out to discuss their experience. He is apologetic and offers Sally a replacement meal. She's not really in the mood for dinner anymore, but accepts the offer. Once Billy and Sally leave the restaurant, they discuss their experience and decide that they won't return to the restaurant.

The same applies when being in a bad relationship. We like what we see on the outside, (the person's physical appearance), and we go into the restaurant (spend time getting to know them). We order drinks and food (become invested in the other person's life), and when the meal finally arrives, it is tainted (find subtle hints and cracks in their personality). Once you have been exposed to the bad experiences, you must communicate your dissatisfaction. If Billy and Sally hadn't mention their bad experience to the waiter and manager, the restaurant would have believed that it was providing a great service.

Communication is key. When you open up about your bad experience, you have to pay attention to how the person responds. Are they compliant? Do they want to change their bad behaviour? Are they apologetic? Or are they defensive and refuse to change? What your partner decides to do about the issue will tell you what the future of that relationship holds.

Whatever type of abuse you have suffered, you can turn your life around. You do not need to stay in a toxic relationship, or accept abusive behaviour from anyone. No one can force you to do anything. No one can take your power, so don't give it away.

You may come across those who do not respect your boundaries. This could mean they have intentions to control you, or that they are unfamiliar with accepting boundaries because they never learned about boundaries during their childhood. If someone is angry with you for setting boundaries, don't take responsibility for their anger. Sympathise with them, but do not compromise your boundaries. Sticking to your boundaries can reveal a person's true colours. To practice boundary-setting, you must have a safety net of people who love and care about you, and who will accept your "No". Remember, people who love you, will love your "No" just as much as your "Yes".

Setting a boundary

Once you have identified something that makes you unhappy or uncomfortable, you set a boundary by informing the other person that you won't accept a certain behaviour and outlining clearly what will happen once they have crossed your boundary. Communicating your boundary is not a means to control. It is a tool to protect yourself. You cannot stop people from behaving a certain way, but you can protect yourself by adding consequences. If you do not enforce a boundary, then it's not a boundary.

Examples

A new relationship has started between Joe and Amy. Amy sets a boundary when it comes to infidelity. She tells Joe that if he cheats on her, she will end the relationship. Joe accepts that if he chooses to sleep with another woman, Amy will break up with him.

Brittney's aunt has emotional outbursts. She humiliates Brittney and makes her feel bad about gaining a few pounds. Brittney confronts her aunt, and calmly says, "Aunt, I do not approve of the way you are speaking to me. I will remove myself from this situation if you continue to belittle me." When Brittney's aunt continues to demean her, Brittney gets up from the couch and leaves her aunt's house.

Sometimes removing yourself from a relationship or friendship opens the other person's eyes to their abusive behaviour. If you choose to stay in the relationship, there is no reason for the other person to reflect on behaviour and uncover their flaws. You cannot change people, but when you set boundaries and enforce consequences, you force them to re-evaluate their behaviour. If they choose to continue their behaviour, it shows that they do not respect you.

Workplace boundaries

Researchers have concluded that one in four people have been bullied in the workplace in their lifetime. According to Smeloans.co.uk. statistically, twenty-three percent of British people have been bullied at work. This is a high number of adults who have felt uncomfortable attending work due to mistreatment.

I have been bullied on two different occasions at different jobs. On both instances, the bully was a manager.

During my twenties I worked as a store assistant in a successful retail store. I was young, insecure and knew very little about myself, and I definitely didn't know anything about applying boundaries in my friendships and relationships. The manager at the time read my body language and thought I was an easy target. She belittled me in front of staff members, shouting at me on the shop floor, frequently hampering my progress by refusing to teach me how to operate the tills, and would purposely choose other members of staff over me to climb the ladder. Other members of staff witnessed her mistreatment of me. I was deemed the black sheep, and no one would support me when I asked for a witness to take my case to human resources. I documented each incident, although it didn't do me any good. One day, the manager shouted at me in front of other staff and customers. Driving home that evening I was crying so hysterically that I nearly caused a car accident. This was the point when I realised that I couldn't allow the bullying to continue because it negatively impacted my life outside of work and sent me into a depression. I quit the job the next day and I felt relieved as soon as I left.

I wouldn't necessarily advise anyone to leave a job without another job lined up if you find yourself in a similar situation to mine. Rather, try to resolve the problem by working through the correct company channels. Speak to an HR advisor or take a colleague with you to confront the bully about their behaviour to see if your situation improves. If it doesn't, you can contact ACAS, (The Advisory, Conciliation and Arbitration Service) a free resource that will discuss your options with you.

If this route isn't an option for you, and you can't or don't want to leave before securing other employment, you can study, expand your skills, and look for a job where you can put your new skills to work.

Transference in the workplace

Children of unsupportive caregivers can sometimes have trouble with managers when they enter the workforce. Strained relationships with parents/caregivers can transfer to the manager/employee relationship. In psychology this is called transference. The term transference means that your feelings for one person are redirected to someone else.

According to HAVOCA (Help for Adult Victims Of Child Abuse) "during transference, people turn into a 'biological time machine'. A nerve is struck when someone says or does something that reminds you of your past. This creates an 'emotional time warp' that transfers your emotional past and your psychological needs into the present."

Oftentimes people who have strained relationships with parents/caregivers mistake their bosses as being mean or cruel when they are being told to do something, because something about the instruction or the way the manager behaves while delivering the instruction, strongly reminds the person of something unpleasant in their past. Transference is most often triggered when the boss is unhappy with your work. Their tone of voice, body language, or something else very subtle can take you back, subconsciously, to a time when your parent/caregiver criticised or chastised you. Those feelings rush back to you and you transfer them to your boss.

There are memories embedded in the subconscious. When you experience a similar negative experience it evokes the feelings you encountered a similar situation.

To deal with these triggers, you first have to acknowledge them, and then take a step back from your current situation to look at it objectively. Is your boss really being mean and unfair, or are you taking the criticism too personally?

Transference doesn't negate the need for boundaries in the workplace. It is still very important to set and defend your boundaries, but if you know you suffer from transference, you have to work a little bit harder to identify whether someone is testing a boundary or you're experiencing transference.

Sexual abuse

Predators who commit sexual assault usually hold power over their victim. The attacker's intension is to take away their victim's control and to dominate their victim with force. Sexual assault of any kind is unpleasant and no one deserves this type of treatment. Sexual assault victims often lose their sense of control, especially if they endure assault by someone they love on a regular basis. But this doesn't mean that they cannot reclaim their power. It takes hard work to build up self-confidence and self-esteem, but with both of these personality traits firmly in place, victims can become survivors.

If you are experiencing ongoing sexual or physical abuse, and you're able to do so safely, you should immediately remove yourself from the situation. Don't return until you're certain that your abuser has really, legitimately changed. If you cannot leave without putting yourself or your children in danger, consult in a family member, a friend, the police, or a suitable organisation that will help get you safety.

Here are some things that you can do to help get you out of a dangerous environment.

- ⊙ Create an escape plan. Get trusted friends and family members to help if you can

- ⊙ Use a hidden recording device to collect evidence of the abuse that can be shown to the police

- ⊙ Keep copies of abusive texts, emails and letters

- ⊙ Keep a detailed record of any injuries suffered as a result of abuse

- ⊙ Report injuries to your GP so they can log the abuse

- ⊙ Hide your savings so you can financially support yourself when you leave

- ⊙ Find out your legal housing rights. Speak with a solicitor if possible

- ⊙ Confide in someone you trust about the intention of leaving your home. Once you have left the property they can keep an eye on the perpetrator if necessary

- ⊙ Contact a charity/helpline that can help meet your needs when you leave home

- ⊙ If you need help from the police, request that officers wear normal clothing when they visit you, so it doesn't cause suspicions

- ⊙ Ask the police for advice in making your home environment safer

- Join a support group, either online or in person

- Find emergency accommodation with friends and/or relatives in case you need to leave home in a hurry

- Carry a list of emergency numbers

- Keep copies of important documents (eg: passport, birth certificate, court orders) in a safe place

- Research which court orders are suitable for your circumstances (eg: injunction, restraining order)

Things to consider for future reference

➤ *Decide what your limits are when it comes to your physical, emotional, spiritual and financial life.*

➤ *Think about what you will and will not allow yourself to be a part of from now on.*

➤ *Reflect upon what you will no longer accept.*

➤ *From now on, what consequence will you set?*

➤ *What will be your boundaries going forward?*

Remember: Teach people how to treat you by setting boundaries

And…..

A healthy relationship is one where both parties respect, value and are considerate of each other's boundaries. If a boundary has been crossed, both parties address and resolve the issue safely.

Chapter 10

Forgiveness

"Forgiveness is a gift you give yourself."

-Suzanne Somers

According to the *Greater Good Magazine*, forgiveness is defined as "a conscious, deliberate decision to release feelings of resentment or vengeance toward a person or group who has harmed you, regardless of whether they actually deserve your forgiveness."

Forgiving someone doesn't mean that you deny how seriously you were hurt, both emotionally and physically. It doesn't mean that you condone or excuse the abusive behaviour. And it doesn't mean that you will forget what you have suffered. And while forgiving someone can help repair a relationship, it doesn't automatically mean that you have to continue the relationship.

According to Mayo Clinic, a non-profit organisation committed to clinical practice, education and research, providing expert care, there are a lot of health and mental health benefits associated with forgiveness. It reduces stress, anger, blood pressure, depression and anxiety. It helps improve relationships and social support. It improves cardiovascular health and supports a healthier immune system.

Forgiveness is a process; it can take a long time to heal. As you start the process, you need to ask yourself some hard questions.

- Which of your past behaviours do you want to change?

- What early signs of a controlling and/or abusive personality did you miss?

- How did you present yourself in the situation?

- What kept/is keeping you in the situation?

- What can you do to move forward?

- What did you learn from this situation that will help you in the future?

- What will you do to prevent yourself from repeating the situation?

Forgiving someone who has hurt you deeply is easier said than done, but it is something you need to do if you want to be truly happy. The techniques in this chapter will help you move toward your healing process.

My experience of forgiveness started when I was in hospital being treated for angina, a condition that caused decreased blood flow to the heart. I felt like a vice was squeezing my chest. I feared that I only had a short time left to live. It was then that I made an attempt to contact my mother, to make peace with her. I knew my illness was heavily associated with carrying feelings of hostility toward her for many years. With the illness appearing out of nowhere, I realised that day that it was caused by years of negative feelings stored inside of me that manifested into a physical illness. At that point I knew that I couldn't continue holding on to my animosity because it would shorten my life.

Revenge

It's not beneficial for you to seek revenge as this will only make matters worse. Instead, let life repay your abuser's bad actions. The bible scripture Romans 12:19 states, "Dear friends, never take revenge. Leave that to the righteous anger of God. For the Scriptures say, 'I will take revenge.' I will pay them back says the Lord. Instead, if your enemies are hungry, feed them. If they are thirsty, give them something to drink. In doing this, you will heap burning coals of shame on their heads". This scripture explains that we are to be the better person and our forgiving actions will make the other person feel ashamed and hopefully recognise that they were wrong. Sometimes the perpetrator isn't remorseful. But that shouldn't affect your decision to forgive them.

Below are useful exercises to help you move toward forgiving your abuser.

Reveal

This is the crucial step toward healing. Whatever you have faced, you must reveal it. Talk to a counsellor, a trusted friend or relative. Tell them, in detail, about the abuse you have suffered. Or write a letter to your abuser without sending it to them. This often helps people to heal.

Start by writing down your experiences here. What happened to you?

_____

_____

_____

_____

_____

_____

_____

Release

You need to let your emotions out. Scream, cry, punch a pillow, or throw it across the room to release your anger. Take deep breaths and acknowledge that you are no longer a victim; you are a survivor! If you are spiritual or hold a religious belief, you can pray or meditate for healing. If you have written the letter to your abuser, you can burn the letter or find another way to destroy it. Imagine the person who harmed you enters a hot air balloon. Watch the balloon rise off the ground, removing that person from your life as it heads further into the air and over the horizon. Wave the balloon goodbye.

Who do you need to release from your heart and your life? What emotions do associate with them?

_____

_____

_____

_____

_____

_____

_____

Repair

The hurt that you are feeling won't disappear overnight, but if you make use of the examples provided it will slowly leave you over time. Acknowledge your feelings. Acknowledge the person who hurt you. Bundle this all up and then let it go with the words, "I release you." You may need to repeat this daily, or even multiple times a day.

Remind yourself that you no longer are in your abuser's hands, and that you are building a happy future for yourself. Remember that releasing the person is for your benefit, not theirs.

Once you have completed this stage, you are on your way to breaking free from the chains of your past.

Remember that nobody is perfect and many people are still dealing with their own issues. You still face the possibility of being disappointed, rejected or offended or hurt – it's part of being human. So forgiving and mentally releasing others is a beneficial exercise for you to repeat throughout your lifetime.

What steps will you take toward healing?

_____

_____

_____

_____

_____

_____

_____

Forgiving yourself

The process of forgiveness is not complete until you forgive yourself – it will take time to accept what has happened but try your best to let it go. Do not blame yourself for any abuse that you endured. Learn from the experience and figure out ways to avoid the same situation in the future.

During the stage of forgiveness, avoid the temptation to ruminate on your abuse, by which I mean don't keep bringing up memories and allowing them to make you feel bad. Don't beat yourself up by wondering what might have happened if you had acted differently. You can't change the past, but you can build a bright future if you are able to process your past.

In the blank spaces below write down all the things that you are finding hard to forgive yourself for, and then write down how you can change your mind-set. For example: I am angry for allowing this person to enter my life and deceive me. You can change the mind-set by saying: I didn't know they were going to do that to me, but I have learned from the situation by becoming wiser.

_____

_____

_____

_____

_____

_____

The change of mindset

Remember: An empowered person learns life's lessons. And a victim endures life's pain.

Chapter 11

Building Your Self Esteem

"No one is you and that is your superpower."

-Anonymous

People with low self-esteem often have a poor self-image. The creation of your self-image starts with your experiences during childhood. Achievements, failures, mistakes, and treatment, both good and bad by others, all contribute to your self-image. It can change over the course of your life, and the exercises listed in this chapter will help you to create a positive one.

Self-esteem describes a person's overall subjective sense of personal worth, how much you like yourself irrespective of the circumstances. It is not based on other people's opinions or how they treat you. Self-esteem is the ability to love and accept yourself for who you are.

If you base your self-esteem on external things, such as an expensive car, a good-looking partner, or what others think of you, you will find it difficult to maintain high self-esteem. These things are fleeting. The car could be involved in an accident. The partner could leave. People could change their opinion of you.

Your value needs to come from within. Regardless of race, skin colour, employment status, job title, financial stability, physical appearance, education, gender, or sexual orientation, all humans have value. We all have talents, gifts and abilities to help and serve one another.

Low self-esteem is based on beliefs that people carry with them due to bad experiences. Women whose partners cheated on them believe that they are ugly. Someone whose teacher humiliated them in front of the class may believe that they are stupid.

We looked at the stories that you have been carrying with you in Chapter 8. How you think and feel about yourself largely determines the quality of your life. Try to reflect on the stories you have developed about yourself and other people.

Remember: Every human being is already worthy, without the validation of others.

Below are a number of exercises to help you build up your self-esteem.

Recognise and acknowledge your thoughts daily.

Write down the thoughts that you have been carrying with you. For example: I am not good enough, or I feel ugly. Write at least 10 things that you have thought about yourself in the past month.

1.

2

3

4

5

_____

_____

_____

_____

_____

_____

6

_____

_____

_____

_____

_____

_____

7

8

9

10

Mark the negative thoughts with a cross and the positive thoughts with a tick. Now examine what you have been telling yourself. Are you setting yourself up for success or failure? If your thoughts are mostly negative, you can make the choice right now to change the narrative of your thoughts for the better.

Self-esteem and intellect

It is obvious that everyone is different by the way we look, behave and sound. The same applies to our intelligence. We all have different strengths and weaknesses. For example, someone can be intelligent academically, while another person shows their intelligence by easily learning to play musical instruments. And yet other people can express their intelligence through art. Throughout your self-esteem journey, you must find out where your strengths and weaknesses lie. When you're aware what your strengths are, you shouldn't feel the need to compare yourself to others, or feel inadequate, because you will realise that everyone is intelligent in their own way.

As you build up your self-image and self-esteem, you need to acknowledge a negative thought as it enters your mind, and change the narrative. Here are some examples of how you can turn your negative thoughts into positive ones.

Limiting beliefs	Rational thinking
My boyfriend cheated on me. I must be ugly	*Tommy cheated, but that does not reflect my attractiveness. He didn't see my worth. I want to be in a relationship with someone who will value me.*
I have lost my job. I must be stupid	*I have lost my job, but I have skills and I can learn more skills. I will find another job that I will enjoy.*
I have done lots of bad things. I'm not a good person.	*I have made mistakes, but I have learned from them and I'm willing to do better.*
My mother has abused me. I must not have any value.	*My mother has treated me badly, but this doesn't reflect my worth.*
I need to be a people-pleaser for others to like me.	*Those who truly love me will not expect me to be at their beck and call.*

The examples above reflect that our negative thought patterns aren't true and we need to challenge these thoughts when we have them. When you think that you are not good enough, reflect on a time when you were proud of something you achieved. If you think that you are unlovable, remember a time when you felt safe and loved. The more often you replace a negative thought with a positive one, the easier it will be for you to believe the best about yourself.

Chart your guilt, fear and criticism

When you fill out this table, you will start to see how much negativity you have been living with.

In each column, write down the things you fear, feel guilty for, and all the criticisms you have told yourself.

Fear	Guilt	Critical
Example: *I fear losing my loved one.*	*I feel guilty for lying to my friend.*	*I have been telling myself how ugly I look every day, and complain about my weight.*

Once you have completed the chart, change the script with *positive affirmations.*

For example:

- **I fear losing a loved one.** You can change your thoughts by saying, "My loved one is still here with me, and I will enjoy every moment with them. Whatever happens, I will be okay, because I have support around me."

- **I feel guilty for lying to my friend.** This statement can be turned into a positive by saying, "I lied to my friend, but next time I will tell the truth."

- **I have been telling myself how ugly I look every day, and complain about my weight.** You can change this by saying, "I will stop saying negative things about myself because I have so much to offer. I commit to losing weight to improve my self-image and self-esteem."

When you have high self-esteem, you are more likely to:

- Maintain healthy relationships and less likely to stay in unhealthy ones

- Be confident when making decisions

- Have positive mental health

- Be resilient and confident

- Have a healthy immune system

- Have a better quality of life

- And you are less likely to be overcritical of yourself and others.

- ⊙ Meanwhile, low self-esteem causes:

- ⊙ Depression

- ⊙ Anxiety

- ⊙ Anger

- ⊙ Guilt

- ⊙ Chronic pain

- ⊙ Immunosuppression

Building your self-esteem is definitely possible. To start, complete the exercises below.

Write down all of your accomplishments, the small as well as the big.

_____

_____

_____

_____

_____

Write down what you like about yourself and the positive aspects of your character. (Ask friends for help if you struggle with this one.)

Write down the challenges you have overcome (eg: completing a course, getting through a tough divorce, supporting a friend /relative through their illness, or overcoming an illness yourself)

⊙ **Stand in front of the mirror and repeat these affirmations for two or three minutes every day.** (Hearing is believing. You will eventually believe the positive affirmations when you repeat it daily.)

- I am great

- I am powerful

- I deserve more

- I am worthy

- I love me, and I am loved

- I deserve respect

- I inspire and impact others positively

- I am beautiful

- I am enough

⊙ **Unfollow social media accounts that make you feel bad about yourself**

- **Practise self-care by:**

- Exercising

- Taking a long bath

- Learning something new

- Taking care of your appearance

- Treating yourself to spa treatments or anything that makes you feel good

- Buying a new outfit

- Eating healthy

- Spending time with people who love you

- Trying things that take you out of your comfort zone

- Indulging your passions (eg volunteering for the homeless or playing an instrument)

- Getting enough sleep

Character reflection table

This table contains personality traits that are considered the qualities of a well-adjusted person. Fill out this table at the beginning of your journey to living free from abuse.

For each trait, think about how strongly it applies to you and then score yourself from 1 to 10. 1 = doesn't really apply to me. 10 = applies strongly.

Personality trait	1	2	3	4	5	6	7	8	9	10
Patient										
Humble										
Thoughtful										
Non judgmental										
Loving										
Honest										
Integrity										
Forgiving										
Empathetic										
Self-controlled										
Disciplined										
Good listener										
Optimistic										
Generous										
Helpful										
Sociable										
Caring										
Reliable										
Trusting										
Responsible										

Come back to this table when you have achieved a free and fulfilling life and see how much you have changed.

Here are different qualities that you can choose to live by to build your character. Which of these would you like to cultivate in your personality?

Circle them.

Kind	Honest	Thoughtful	Appreciative	Caring
Creative	Trustworthy	Loyal	Strong	Assertive
Responsible	Friendly	Polite	Reliable	Respectful
Forgiving	Bold	Self-controlled	Eloquent	Focused
Confident	Empathetic	Disciplined	Organised	Punctual
Ambitious	Independent	Great listener	Encouraging	Generous
God fearing	Graceful	Self-expressive	Decisive	Gentle
Content	Loving	Humble	Courageous	Patient

Train your brain to believe that you are, for instance, organised, and follow this up with actions.

Below are 10 actions from my own life which I hope will help boost your self-esteem. These need to be practiced daily if you wish to see a change in your self-perception. Remember things don't happen overnight, you will build them up steadily.

1. **Set goals and work towards them daily**. Write down 50 things that you want to accomplish in your life. At the back of this book in chapter 15, I have created a goal sheet so you can take up the challenge.

2. **Genuinely compliment others.** When you compliment someone, it makes you feel good that you have made someone else feel good.

3. **Be kind to others**. This can be as small as listening to someone. Give someone a hug. Or do someone a favour. When you are

kind to others, it immediately makes you feel good.

4. **Go easy on yourself when you have made a mistake**. Remember, you are human and no one is perfect! We all fail sometimes, and loving yourself unconditionally means forgiving yourself when you make a mistake. What would you say to your child who made a mistake? Would you still love them? Treat yourself the same way.

5. **Focus on your positive qualities.** Banish negative thoughts because you have so many more positive attributes to reflect on than the negative. Each time you have a negative thought about yourself, challenge it and change it to a positive statement.

6. **Forgive yourself for the past.** Whatever happened, don't be hard on yourself. Realise that everyone makes mistakes and you are willing to learn from the situation to be better for the future.

7. **Practice gratitude.** Spend five minutes a day thinking about the things that you are thankful for – being employed, good health, a roof you have over your head, a supportive friend. Continue adding things to the list and you will see a change in your self-esteem.

8. **Turn your negative experience into a positive one** by focusing on the positive things in your life. Having a victor's mindset will help you through those difficult times.

9. **Add joy to your life.** Do things that make you happy. Walk your dog. Bake a cake. Call your best friend for a catch up. Doing things you enjoy will increase life satisfaction.

10. **Pray and meditate.** Praying to a higher power brings peace to

most people and makes them feel worthy. Other health benefits include reduced anxiety, increased happiness, enhanced self-awareness, and reduced stress.

Here is a sample list of some of the most popular professions, titles and qualities of character. Tick all of the boxes that describe who you are. So, for example, if you are a mother who is employed and you have an encouraging personality, you can tick the relevant boxes

Below is an explanation of the exercise.

☐ Friend	☐ Surgeon
☐ Care taker	☐ Mechanic
☐ Teacher	☐ Plumber
☐ Dinner lady	☐ Employer
☐ Doctor	☐ Optician
☐ Pastor	☐ Beauty therapist
☐ Cleaner	☐ Solicitor
☐ Banker	☐ Nursery nurse
☐ Administrator	☐ Nurse
☐ Gym Instructor	☐ Entertainer
☐ Business person	☐ Partner
☐ Carer	☐ Smiler
☐ Mother	☐ Encourager

☐ Dustbin man   ☐ Listener

☐ Family member   ☐ Helper

☐ Employee   ☐ Shop keeper

☐ Counsellor   ☐ Caring

☐ Father   ☐ Kind

☐ Driver   ☐ Understanding

☐ Builder   ☐ Inventor

☐ Nurse   ☐ Philanthropist

☐ Roofer

Notice that all of these titles and qualities, whether they relate to formal employment or not, address a need to another person. These titles, whether low or high in category, are of benefit to everyone within society. Therefore, there shouldn't be any judgment based on what is perceived to hold a higher rank. Everyone provides a service that is of need.

Examples

A cleaner makes a home, school and offices clean for other people to stay in a hygienic environment.

A counsellor supports, listens and encourages people throughout their hardships to help them back on track.

Reflect on the service you do for others, even if you're unemployed. Think of the kind things you have done for others, such as being a supportive friend or family member. These acts of service, whether great or small, make a difference in other people's lives.

Don't let anyone else define your worth. Build up such a strong positive mental image of yourself that other people's opinions cannot impact you. Celebrate your uniqueness. Look at the great qualities you possess. Be a positive influence in this world

Once your lifestyle and mind-set have positively changed, you will start attracting the right people into your life.

Remember: Your inner world reflects your outer world.

Chapter 12

Recognise Toxic Characteristics In Others

"The quality of your life is the quality of your relationships"

-Tony Robbins

Building up your self-esteem, while completely worthwhile, can take some time. But exposing yourself to toxic people can set your progress back to square one if you're not careful. To avoid being mistreated by someone new, be vigilant about the person's behaviour while you are getting to know them.

To have a healthy relationship with someone else, you must first have a healthy relationship with yourself. How you feel about yourself impacts your relationships. It's also imperative to find someone who has a healthy relationship with themselves, if they dislike themselves their issues may impact you. They must have respect for themselves, examples of this is, listening to what they say about themselves. Do they hold themselves in high esteem or do they put themselves down? What is their body language like when they walk around? You must look out for tell-tale signs of how a person treats themselves. It will give you an example of their self-perception.

Throughout the 30 years of abuse I have suffered, I have analysed a number of circumstances where I have created a questionnaire to screen the person's character. You can use these questions to evaluate your new relationships or friendships to gain more perspective. Answer the questions below, and if you find that the answers are negative, you need to carefully consider if you want to remain in the relationship. If you do, you need to speak openly and honestly with the other person. Discuss the problems and see if the underlying issues can be resolved.

Behaviour in public

- How do they treat people in public?

- How do they treat the waitress when they are being served?

- How do they treat or view homeless people?

Their attitude toward yourself

- How do they speak to you?

- How do they describe you as a person?

- Are they appreciative of your time?

- Do they message or call you in a healthy, consistent way?

- Do they plan to see you on a consistent basis?

- Do they support you emotionally when you need help?

- Do they encourage you to be a better person?

- Are they interested in learning about you?

- Do they support your dreams and visions?

- Do they celebrate your achievements?

- Do they talk about themselves a lot and not ask about you?

- Do they listen to your advice?

- Do they show signs of jealousy or possessiveness towards you? *If so, this is not a good sign. This behaviour usually leads to a coercive, controlled relationship down the line*

- Do they spontaneously surprise you with a treat?

- Do they stare at attractive women or men in front of you, making you feel inferior?

- Do they respect your values and beliefs?

- Do they respect your boundaries?

- Are they critical of you?

- If you have a good relationship with your family and friends, what do they think about the person?

- Do they open up to you about everything, or are they holding back information about their lives?

- Do they moan or discourage you to spend time with your friends or family?

- Do they compliment you or do they put you down with your appearance?

- Do they leave you out or do they include you to outings?

Attitude toward friends and family

- Do they have friends?

- If they don't have friends, why? And who are they close to?

- Are they capable of holding long-lasting friendships?

- How do they speak to their friends and family?

- How do they behave among their friends and family?

- What do their friends and family say about them?

- Are they respectful of your friends and family?

Their ambitions

- Do they have ambitions?

- Are they actively pursuing their dreams?

- Are they financially stable?

- Do they work?

- What is their outlook on life?

- Are they happy with where they are in their life?

- If they aren't happy, what are they doing to change for the better?

- Do they take responsibility for where they are in life?

- Do they blame others for their misfortunes?

- Do they include you when they discuss future plans?

Their outlook

- What have they said their childhood was like?

- Have they been hurt before and have they forgiven the person?

- Do they look after their appearance?

- What do they spend majority of their time doing?

- Have they been open about past relationships?

- Are they emotionally mature?

- Do they take responsibility for themselves or do they make excuses?

- Do they respect other people's cultures and beliefs?

- What is their definition of love?

- Does integrity mean a lot to them or not?

- Do they keep their promises?

- Do they have religious beliefs, and do they practice them?

- Is their level of hygiene good?

- What are their thoughts on and expectations about marriage?

- If they want to get married, what is their timeline for getting married?

⊙ Are they reliable/do they cancel on you often?

⊙ Do they compare your success with theirs?

⊙ Are they trustworthy?

Their attitude towards finances

⊙ Do they gamble?

⊙ Do they have debt and how much?

⊙ What do they spend majority of their money on?

⊙ Do they spend or save their money?

⊙ Would they offer help if you're in need financially?

⊙ Do they have financial goals?

Violence

⊙ Are they quickly angered?

⊙ Do they watch a lot of violent programmes?

⊙ Do they own weapons that concern you?

⊙ Have you ever witnessed them under pressure? How do they cope?

⊙ How do they react in a volatile situation? If you do not know, then how do they say they would react?

- Do they consume narcotics or drink a lot of alcohol?

- Do they have addictions of any kind?

- Do they harm animals?

- Do their surroundings show they are violent? *(eg* holes in the walls where they punched it.)

- Have they been in fights before?

- Have they been to prison before? If so what for?

Their children and exes

- Do they want children?

- If they want kids, how many? And is their number the same/similar to yours?

- When do they want to have children? Is it in the same/similar timeline as yours?

- What are their opinions on child rearing?

- If they have children, what is their relationship with the other parent? Does it appear healthy or unhealthy?

- Do they provide for their children?

- Do they spend time with their children?

- If they don't have children, are they still friends with their exes?

- What are their opinions about remaining friends with exes?

⊙ If you have children, how do they treat them?

If the answers to these questions are unsettling or concerning, it would be prudent to closely evaluate your relationship. Especially if you notice them change drastically a few weeks into the relationship. If they are kind and considerate at the start of the relationship, but become mean and cruel a few weeks or months later, chances are that you ignored, or missed, the signs of their true personality earlier. It's no use to scrutinise every moment, but it is a good idea to watch the person's life from a distance. Time will definitely reveal their true colours.

Insecurities

Like attracts like. An insecure person will attract another insecure person. Your thoughts enter your subconscious and you will act those thoughts. Your energy and behaviour are magnets that will attract people similar to you.

Everyone has insecurities, but high levels of insecurity can put others off. If you deal with your issues, work through and resolve them, you will get much more joy and fulfilment from a relationship. Unresolved issues and insecurities will come to the surface, no matter how hard you try to hide them. If you take your insecurities into a new relationship, depending on the person's personality, you may give your new partner the opportunity of taking advantage of you. If your partner is a good fit for you, your issues could potentially damage the relationship. To give your relationship its best chance of thriving, it's best to talk about the issue to help you move forward. No one is perfect and you don't need to be completely healed to enter a relationship. But it's better to have dealt with a lot of your past, or it will follow you into your relationship, causing destruction.

Remember: Your partner should bring out the best in you.

Chapter 13

Your Outlook Matters

"If you change the way you look at things, the things you look at change."

-Wayne Dyer

In Chapter 11 we explored how your own mental image and outlook affect your life. You wrote down your thoughts. It's now time to look at how you perceive your life. Take a look at this picture. What do you see?

An old woman? A young woman? Take a closer look at the old woman's eye – that's the young woman's ear. The young woman's necklace is the old woman lips. The old woman's chin is the young woman's neck and the old woman's nose is the young woman's chin. Hopefully you are able to see both illusions now.

This image illustrates that you can choose what you want to focus on. In your life, you can choose to see the abuse you have endured as an empowering force that helps you to become a stronger person who has learned from the situation. Or you can choose to be a victim and feel downtrodden. Every circumstance is defined by your perception. Although abuse is bad, you can chose to find something positive in the experience. It's what you do with your life afterwards that matters.

Oprah Winfrey, a business mogul, actress and TV host, is a great example of how perception can mould life.

Oprah's early years were unsteady. Her mother and father were separated and she lived with her grandmother for a few years. Later she moved back and forth between her mother's and father's homes. At age nine, she suffered sexual abuse at the hands of a family member and endured many beatings. She fell pregnant at fourteen, and her baby later died. Regardless of her childhood experiences, her aim was to turn her life around.

In one interview that Oprah gave about childhood trauma she said, "I now know from interviewing over 50,000 people over the years, and my own personal experiences, that everything that has happened to you can be used to strengthen you, if you allow it, if you're open to it. So it's because of my own mistakes, and my own observations about life, and paying attention, that I now can live the most peaceful life of anybody I know. But it has taken work to get here".

Oprah refused to be a victim. She chose to use her experiences to build a great life and impact millions of people's lives. She is a living example that anyone can lead a life of abundance, peace and joy, regardless of past experiences.

Remember: You cannot change the past, but you can change your future.

Chapter 14

It's Never Too Late To Start Again

"Every moment is a fresh beginning."

-T.S Eliot

Although you have been hurt by others, it doesn't mean that everyone will treat you badly. You may be scared to start a new friendship or romantic relationship, but if you pay attention to people's behaviour before getting too emotionally involved, you can stop the cycle of abuse from repeating itself. Try not to live in the past and project your feelings of worry or insecurity onto the other person.

I have two pieces of advice for starting over. Firstly, listen to how you feel, because it's a signal. Pay attention to how you feel daily and question why you feel the way you do. Sometimes your feelings and responses are associated with past experiences and it's good to be aware if you are bringing the past into the present.

Secondly, follow your gut instinct, your intuition. It's there to protect you. If you have ignored it for a long time, make a conscious effort to listen to your gut. If you feel uneasy about a person or situation, be mindful. If someone makes you feel uncomfortable, pay attention to your gut and take appropriate actions. You are a powerful person, never underestimate yourself! We are all connected to a high power – God – and that small inner voice is God speaking to us. Never deny how you are feeling. If it doesn't feel right, it's not right for you.

Our mistakes, failures, and embarrassments are all stepping stones along our path of learning. Learn from them and don't take them into your future. Clinging onto the past heavily impacts our present and future. Remember, if you release the past, it will no longer have power over you. Life is an ongoing journey of forgiving and releasing the past.

Regardless of your mistakes and failings, you are not a bad person. You have value. Remember, no one is perfect. Don't be hard on yourself, but take comfort that you are growing. Most of us are evolving to become better people. Our experiences make us wiser and can mould us to be more empathetic toward others.

It is never too late to start again. If you are free from the abuse, or are in the midst of cutting those off who abuse you, remember that you are valuable. You deserve respect and no one deserves abuse. Breaking free is scary, but once you are free, it is exhilarating to start your life anew. Learning from past mistakes allows you to avoid similar situations in the future. Once you start to love yourself, your future will be bright. You will have a profound new confidence that will attract the right people into your life.

To everyone who has experienced toxic relationships, unsupportive and unloving family members, fake friends and other abusive people, know that you are worthy, beautiful and unique. You have many gifts and abilities, with so much to offer the world. You have come so far and you are still standing. Continue improving yourself and, most of all, accept who you are. Learn from your mistakes and kiss your past goodbye because you're entering a positive chapter in your life. Know your worth and attain all the things you want in your life. You deserve it!

I hope this book has helped you on some level and you now realise that you no longer need to accept what other people do to you. You have a choice; you're in the driver's seat. You have the chance to create a life that makes you happy every single day. Learn to love yourself and never be afraid to start again, because every day can be a new beginning.

Chapter 15

Goal Sheet

"The power to change your life lies in the simplest of steps."

-Steve Maraboli

Now it's time to build yourself up again. In **Chapter 11** it mentioned writing your 50 goals. I have created this goal sheet for you to write all the goals that you have for your life.

To start with, write down 50 things you'd like to achieve in your lifetime.

Goal	Category
1	
2	
3	
4	
5	

6	
7	
8	
9	
10	
11	
12	
13	
14	
15	
16	
17	
18	
19	
20	
21	
22	
23	
24	

25	
26	
27	
28	
29	
30	
31	
32	
33	
34	
35	
36	
37	
38	
39	
40	
41	
42	
43	

44	
45	
46	
47	
48	
49	
50	

The next step is to categorise your priority. Go back to your list and add the relevant letter into the category column

M = Mental health

P = Physical health

R = Relationships

F = Finances

L = Lifestyle

Next, rank your goals in order of importance to you in each category. (eg: losing weight for physical health might be more important to you than to quit smoking.)

Now break down each goal into all of the small steps you need to achieve that goal (eg: going to the gym three times a week and being strict with your eating habits.)

Keep this goal sheet handy and complete one step from each category a day. Give yourself a time frame of when you expect to accomplish them.

Before you know it, you will achieve your goals and can celebrate each accomplishment and you will be able to tick it off your list.

Mental health

Goal	Steps
1	
2	

3

4

5

Physical health

Goal	Steps
1	

2

3

4

5

Relationships

Goal	Steps
1	
2	

3

4

5

| | |
| | |

Finances

Goal	Steps
1	

2

3

4

5

Lifestyle

Goal	Steps
1	
2	

3

4

5

Chapter 16

Abuse Helplines

Women

Refuge

National women's and children's domestic abuse helpline

24hrs a day 0808 2000 247

Www.nationalhelpline.org.uk

Website Www.refuge.org.uk

Freedom charity

For women and young people

Www.freedomcharity.org.uk

247 helpline 0845 607 0133

You can text for help, text the words 4freedom: to 88802

Live fear free

An organisation that provides advice against violence, domestic abuse and sexual violence

Www.gov.wales/live-fear-free

Email info@livefearfreehelpline.wales

Text 07860077333

247 Helpline 0808 801 0800

South hall black sisters

Is a non-profit organisation that supports back and Asian ethnic group with all types of abuse.

Www.southhallblacksisters.org.uk

0208 571 9595

Mon-Fri 9am -5pm

FCO The Forced marriage unit

Www.Fmu@fco.gov.uk

020 7008 0151 or 0044 20 7008 0151 for overseas

Sharan project south Asian women help support

Www.Sharan.org.uk

0844 504 3231

Office hours Monday –Friday 9.30am-5pm

The freedom programme

Www.freedomprogramme.co.uk

01942 262 270

Help@freedomprogramme.co.uk

Designed to help women to escape the pattern of abuse. Also can be for men who are perpetrators to help them stop abusing.

Women's aid

An organisation that supports women and children who experience domestic abuse

Www.womensaid.org.uk

Email helpline@womensaid.org.uk

General enquiries info@womensaid.org.uk

Young people

The Hide out

Website for children and young people witnessing domestic violence.

Www.thehideout.org.uk

Supportline

Children & young people support

Www.Supportline.org.uk

Email info@supportline.org.uk

Helpline 01708 765 200 *(Hours vary so ring for details)*

Young minds

Helpline for young people.

Www.Youngminds.org.uk

0808 802 5544

Text YM to 85258

Open 247

Childline under 19s

Www.Childline.org.uk

0800 11 11

Available 247

Men

Safeline

Www.safeline.org.uk

A charity that supports men who have experienced sexual abuse.

Helpline 01926 402 498

-counselling

-sexual violence advisor

National male survivor helpline 0808 800 5005

Monday 9am-5pm

Tuesday 8am-8pm

Wednesday 9am-5pm

Thursday 8am-8pm

Friday 9am-5pm

Saturday 10am-2pm

Men's advice line

Www.mensadviceline.org.uk

Info@mensadviceline.org.uk

0808 801 0327

Mon-Fri 9am-8pm

Sat and sun 10am-12pm and 4pm-6pm

Helpline for domestic violence perpetrators 0808 802 4040

Mankind Initiative

A charity for men to help escape domestic abuse.

www.mankind.org.uk

01823 334244 week days between 10am -4pm

Survivors UK

Www.Survivorsuk.org

For adult male survivors of rape or sexual assault.

02035983898

help@survivorsuk.org

Help line webchat Monday –Sunday 12.00-20.00

Office hours 09.30-17.00

Email Info@survivorsuk.org

Other organisations

ACAS

Www.ACAS.org.uk

Helpline 03001231100

Breaking the silence

Http://www.btsuk.org

0121 285 2277

Crime stoppers

A charity that helps people who wants to avoid direct contact with the police.

Www.crimestoppers-uk.org

0800 555111

Victim support helpline

A helpline that supports survivors after a crime

Www.victimsupport.org.uk

0808 168 9111

Last Word

Thank you for reading this book and I hope that you found it useful. Love this book? Don't forget to leave a review! Every review matters, and it matters a *lot!* Head over to Amazon to leave a review for me. Thank you so much.

If you want to get in touch:

Email: nicola-deane@outlook.com

About the Author

Nicola had many people in her life that suffered abuse. Unable to deal with his history of childhood abuse, her father committed suicide.

Her mother has found herself in ongoing unhealthy relationships. Her friends have also suffered abuse at the hands of their family members. With abuse wreaking havoc around her, Nicola is committed to helping men and women break free from the cycle of abuse.

Nicola is in the process of contacting MPs to tighten the laws of injunction and the laws around domestic abuse in the United Kingdom.

References

1. Glenn R. Schiraldi, year PhD, 2007, 10 Simple Solutions for Building Self-esteem

2. * Hay, L. 2008, Mirror Work 21 Days to Heal Your Life

3. * Shapiro F. 2018 Getting Past Your Past, Take Control of Your Life With Self-help Techniques From EDMR Therapy.

4. * Cloud, H. and Townsend, J. 1992 Boundaries Take Control of Your Life

5. * Maxwell Malta, MD, 2015 Psycho Cybernetics

6. * Jampolsky, MD G. 2007 Forgiveness, The Greatest Healer of All

7. * Williams J 2018 How to Analyse People

8. * Mayo Clinic Staff 2020, Forgiveness: Letting Go Of Grudges And Bitterness,

9. *https://www.mayoclinic.org/healthy-lifestyle/adult-health/in-depth/forgiveness/art-20047692

10. *www.thehotline.org "Why Don't They Just Leave?"

11. *https://narcissistabusesupport.com/people-stay-abusive-relationships/

12. * Https://youtu.be/kEzGN39duWg

13. *Making working life better for everyone in Britain https://www.acas.org.uk/

14. * A New Covid-19 Crisis: Domestic Abuse Rises Worldwide

15. *https://www.nytimes.com/2020/04/06/world/coronavirus-domestic-violence.html

16. * Harvey, O 2017, 5 Concerning Things Low Self-esteem Can do to

Your Body *https://hellogiggles.com/lifestyle/health-fitness/things-low-self-esteem-does-to-your-body*

17. * *https://www.refuge.org.uk/*

18. * Rosling, L 2020, ¼ of UK Employees Bullied at Work

19. * *https://www.smeloans.co.uk/blog/bullying-in-the-workplace-statistics-uk/*

20. * Robinson, L & Segal J Ph.D 2021, Help For Men Who Are Being abused

21. * *https://www.helpguide.org/articles/abuse/help-for-men-who-are-being-abused.htm*

22. * Office for National Statistics 2021, Domestic Abuse

23. * *https://www.ethnicity-facts-figures.service.gov.uk/crime-justice-and-the-law/crime-and-reoffending/domestic-abuse/latest*

24. * Fred Luskin's 2021, What is Forgiveness?

25. * https://greatergood.berkeley.edu/topic/forgiveness/definition

26. * The First Step To Freedom From Domestic Abuse

    http://www.google.com/url?sa=t&rct=j&q=&esrc=s&source=web&cd=&ved=2ahUKEwisuOCjnqHyAhWLOsAKHcKqDF4QFnoECAMQAw&url=http%3A%2F%2Fwww.thefirststep.org.uk%2Fwp-content%2Fuploads%2F2015%2F04%2FTypes-of-abuse-and-examples.pdf&usg=AOvVaw02XWbDd0gTFCxox6

27. * Louis de Canonville, C, What is Coercive Control?

    https://narcissticbehavior.net/coercive-control/

28. * United Nations, What is Domestic Abuse?

    https://www.un.org/en/coronavirus/what-is-domestic-abuse

29. *

    https://www.bing.com/images/search?view=detailV2&ccid=sUPstXJe&id=8

Part 3: Begin the Healing

*BCCE0DEA42219F7FB0DFC1F21E9C99FEF5AFF05&thid=OIP.s
UPstXJeddDl_DCc5YWOrQHaHa&mediaurl=https%3A%2F%2Fi5.wal
martimages.com%2Fasr%2F5f526f0c-a880-440a-9209-
024a4be23ae5_1.f42bebf5a30873f75fa09c843545463a.jpeg%3FodnWidth%
3D612%26odnHeight%3D612%26odnBg%3Dffffff&cdnurl=https%3A%2
F%2Fth.bing.com%2Fth%2Fid%2FR.b143ecb5725e75d0e5fc309ce5858ead
%3Frik%3DBf9a75%252fJ6SEf%252fA%26pid%3DImgRaw%26r%3D0
&exph=612&expw=612&q=young+wpman+illusion&simid=608006230
657692343&form=IRPRST&ck=2E27BD9F69FBAD5C30CB013D5
AC927E5&selectedindex=1&ajaxhist=0&ajaxserp=0&vt=2*

https://thefirststep.org.uk/

30 Care Act 2014,

https://www.legislation.gov.uk/ukpga/2014/23/contents/enacte
d

31 Help for Adult Victims of Child Abuse (HAVOCA),

https://www.havoca.org/

32 What is forgiveness, Greater Good magazine,

https://greatergood.berkeley.edu/topic/forgiveness/definition

33 The First Step, To Freedom From Domestic Abuse,

https://thefirststep.org.uk/

Printed in Great Britain
by Amazon